KS2
7–8
Years

Master Maths at Home

Geometry and Shape

Scan the QR code to help your child's learning at home.

 | **MATHS** **NO PROBLEM!**

mastermathsathome.com

How to use this book

Maths — No Problem! created **Master Maths at Home** to help children develop fluency in the subject and a rich understanding of core concepts.

Key features of the Master Maths at Home books include:

- Carefully designed lessons that provide structure, but also allow flexibility in how they're used.

- Speech bubbles containing content designed to spark diverse conversations, with many discussion points that don't have obvious 'right' or 'wrong' answers.

- Rich illustrations that will guide children to a discussion of shapes and units of measurement, allowing them to make connections to the wider world around them.

- Exercises that allow a flexible approach and can be adapted to suit any child's cognitive or functional ability.

- Clearly laid-out pages that encourage children to practise a range of higher-order skills.

- A community of friendly and relatable characters who introduce each lesson and come along as your child progresses through the series.

You can see more guidance on how to use these books at **mastermathsathome.com**.

We're excited to share all the ways you can learn maths!

Maths — No Problem!
mastermathsathome.com
www.mathsnoproblem.com
hello@mathsnoproblem.com

First published in Great Britain in 2022 by
Dorling Kindersley Limited
One Embassy Gardens, 8 Viaduct Gardens, London SW11 7BW
A Penguin Random House Company

The authorised representative in the EEA is Dorling Kindersley
Verlag GmbH. Arnulfstr. 124, 80636 Munich, Germany

10 9 8 7 6 5 4 3 2 1
001–327081–Jan/22

A CIP catalogue record for this book is available from the British Library.

ISBN: 978-0-24153-923-1
Printed and bound in the UK

For the curious
www.dk.com

This book was made with Forest Stewardship Council™ certified paper - one small step in DK's commitment to a sustainable future. For more information go to www.dk.com/our-green-pledge

Acknowledgements

The publisher would like to thank the authors and consultants Andy Psarianos, Judy Hornigold, Adam Gifford and Dr Anne Hermanson.

The Castledown typeface has been used with permission from the Colophon Foundry.

Contents

Ruby   Elliott   Amira   Charles   Lulu   Sam   Oak   Holly   Ravi   Emma   Jacob   Hannah

Making angles

Starter

Look at these letters. Which letter doesn't make an angle?

S A M

Example

An angle is formed when two straight lines meet at a point.

S A M

This A and this M are made of straight lines.

This S has no angles as it is made from one curved line.

4

1 Circle the shapes that have angles.

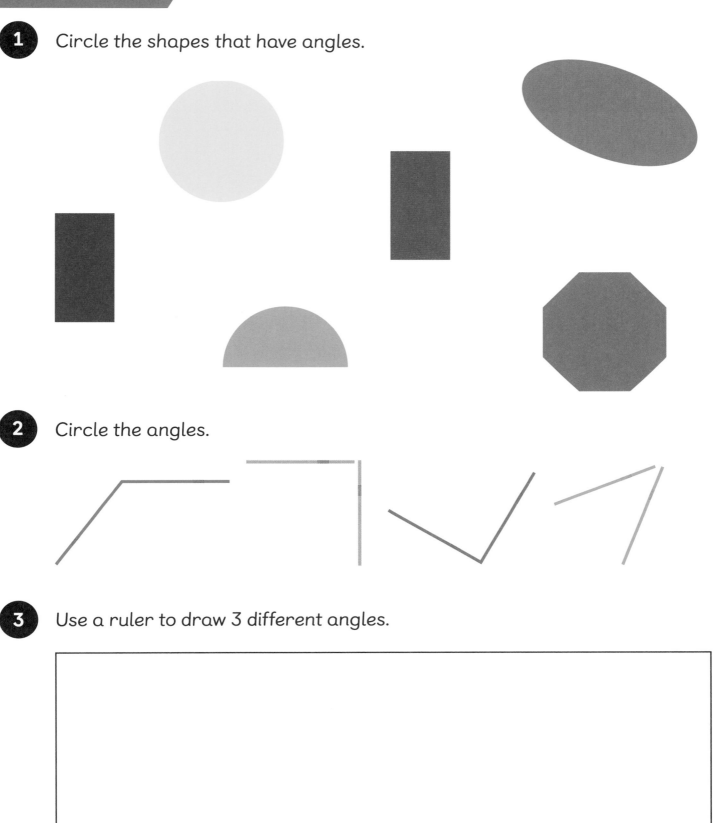

2 Circle the angles.

3 Use a ruler to draw 3 different angles.

Finding angles

Starter

How many angles are inside these shapes?

Example

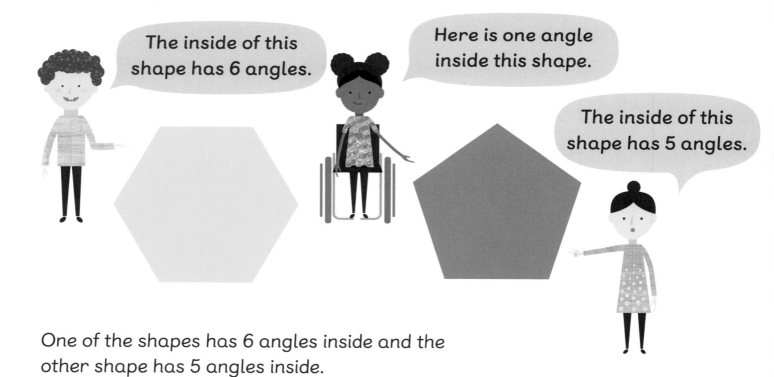

The inside of this shape has 6 angles.

Here is one angle inside this shape.

The inside of this shape has 5 angles.

One of the shapes has 6 angles inside and the other shape has 5 angles inside.

1

This shape has 8 sides.

Circle all the angles you can find in this shape.

2

(a) How many sides does this shape have?

(b) How many angles does it have?

3 Use a ruler to draw one shape that has 4 angles inside and one shape that has 3 angles inside.

Finding right angles

Starter

Sam made a picture of a house using only rectangles.

All the angles in the rectangles are equal. We can also say they are **congruent**.

What types of angles do rectangles have?

Example

All the angles in the picture are the same type.

When two lines meet like this, they make a right angle.

This is how we mark a right angle.

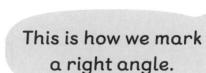

All the angles in a rectangle are right angles.

1 Circle all the right angles.

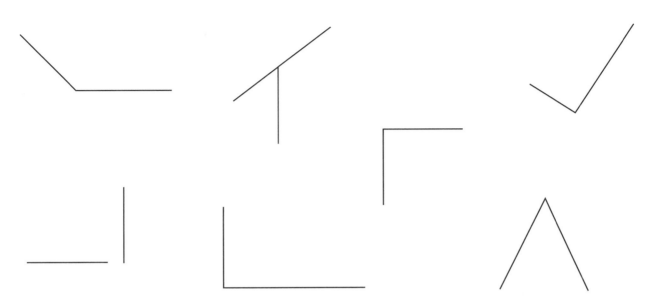

2 Circle the shapes that have right angles.

Comparing angles

Starter

How can we compare these angles?

Example

 used a right-angle checker.

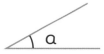

Angle a is smaller than a right angle.

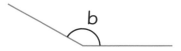

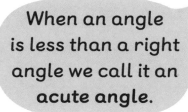 When an angle is less than a right angle we call it an **acute angle**.

Angle b is larger than a right angle.

When an angle is more than a right angle we call it an **obtuse angle**.

Angle c is a right angle.

1 Label the angles as acute, obtuse or right angle.

(a)

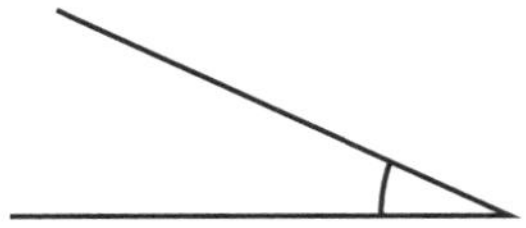

(b)

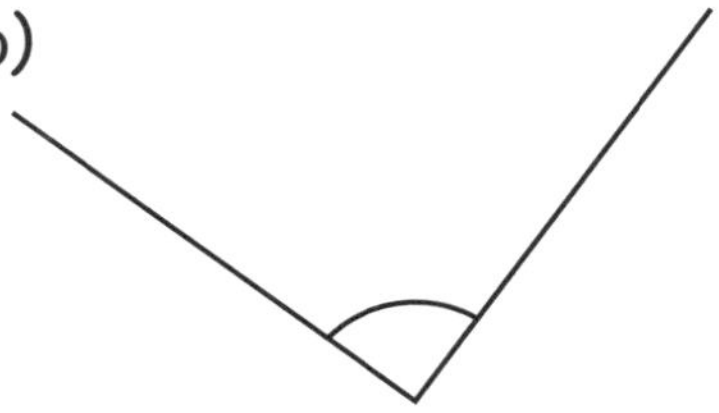

(c)

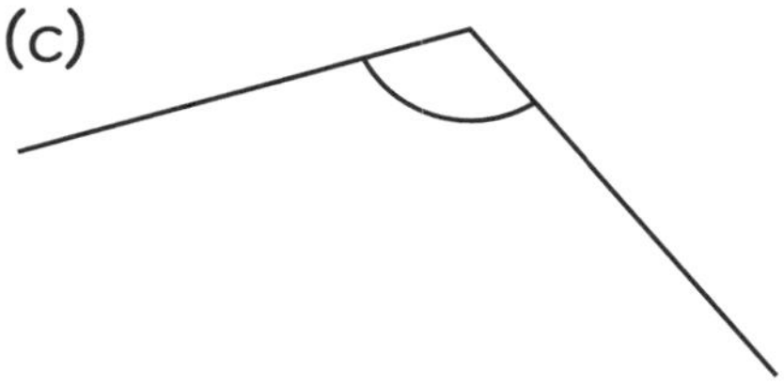

(d)

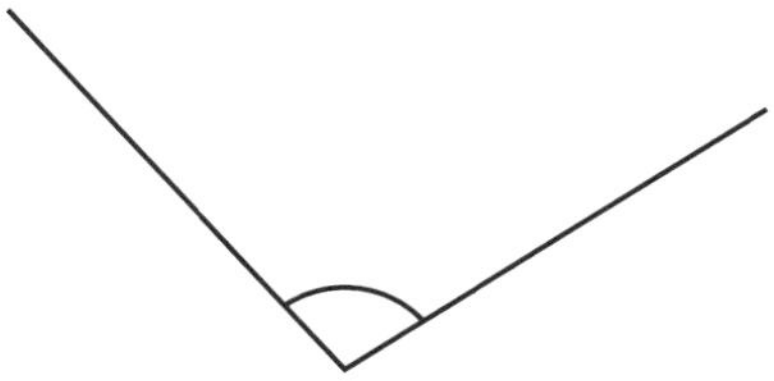

(e)

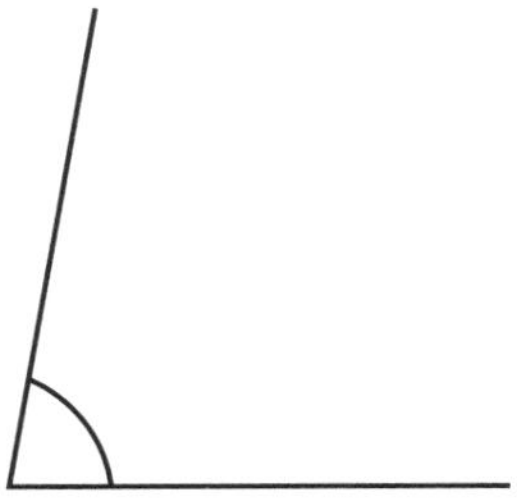

2 (a) Name a shape that has only right angles.

(b) Name a shape that has only acute angles.

(c) Draw a shape that has one obtuse angle and two acute angles.

Making turns

How can Ruby and Elliott turn so they are facing each other?

Example

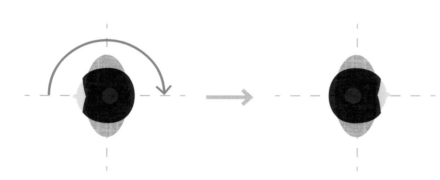

I can make a half turn, clockwise or anticlockwise.

I can make a three-quarter turn clockwise.

I can also make a quarter turn anticlockwise.

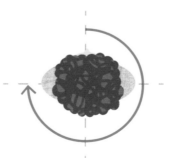

Practice

1 Describe each turn the children make.

(a)

Ruby makes a [   ]

turn [   ].

(b)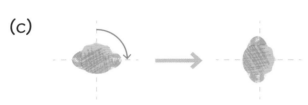

Ravi makes a [   ]

turn [   ].

(c)

Sam makes a [   ]

turn [   ].

2 Draw the position of the arrow after each turn.

(a) half turn

(b) quarter turn clockwise

(c) three-quarter turn anticlockwise

3 Circle the letters that will look the same after a half turn.

A E N O S T X Z

Identifying perpendicular lines

Starter

How can we describe lines AB and BC?

Example

Lines AB and BC meet at a right angle.

Lines that meet at a right angle are perpendicular.

This book has four pairs of perpendicular lines.

Line AB is perpendicular to line BC.

Line AB is perpendicular to line DA.

Line DA is perpendicular to line DC.

Line DC is perpendicular to line CB.

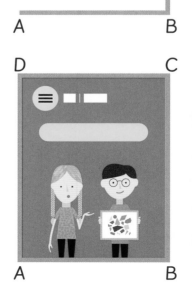

1 Colour the shapes that have perpendicular lines.

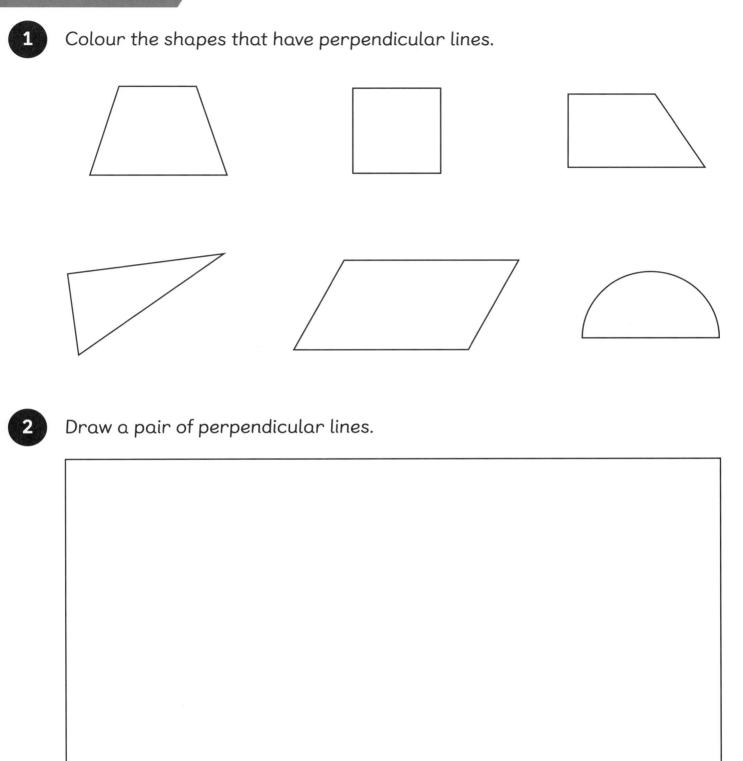

2 Draw a pair of perpendicular lines.

Identifying parallel lines

How can we describe the rungs on this ladder?

This is a rung.

Example

The rungs don't meet at an angle. We call these lines **parallel lines**.

Parallel lines never meet, no matter how far we extend the lines.

If I extend these lines, they will never meet.

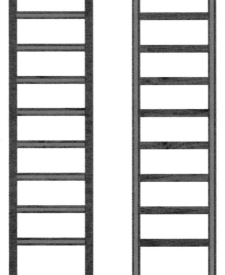

The sides of the ladder are also parallel to each other.

All the rungs of the ladder are parallel to each other.

1   Make a list of some other items with parallel lines.

2   Draw a pair of parallel lines on this grid.

3   Colour the shapes that have parallel lines.

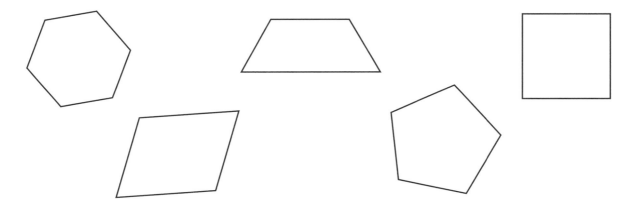

Finding vertical and horizontal lines

Starter

How can we describe the sides of the window?

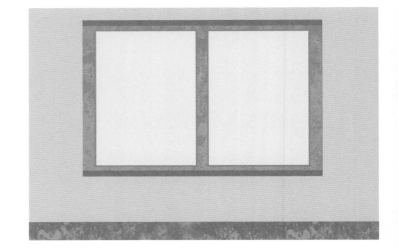

Example

Lines that are parallel to the ground are said to be **horizontal** lines.

Lines that are perpendicular to the ground are said to be **vertical** lines.

Lines AD and BC are both horizontal lines.

Lines AB and DC are both vertical lines.

1

Look at the bookcase and circle the correct word.

(a)   The shelves in the bookcase are (horizontal / vertical).

(b)   The spines of the books are (horizontal / vertical).

(c)   The sides of the bookcase are (horizontal / vertical).

(d)   The top of the bookcase is (horizontal / vertical).

2   Complete these sentences using **horizontal** or **vertical**.

(a) When I stand up I am [   ].

(b) When I lie down in bed I am [   ].

(c) A lamp post is [   ].

(d) A tabletop is [   ].

Describing 2D shapes

How can we describe the lines and angles in this 2D shape?

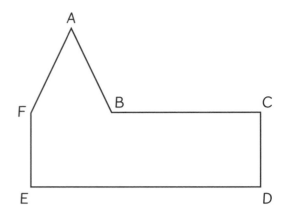

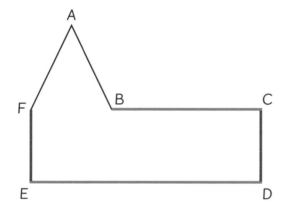

Lines BC and ED are parallel.
Lines FE and CD are parallel.

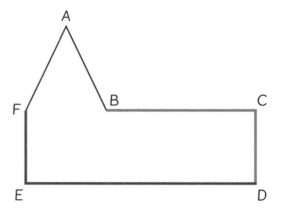

Lines BC and CD are perpendicular.
Lines FE and ED are perpendicular.

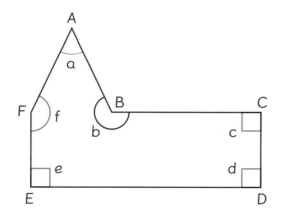

Angle b is bigger than a straight line. We call these **reflex angles**.

Angle a is acute. It is smaller than a right angle.
Angle f is obtuse. It is larger than a right angle.
Angles c, d and e are right angles.

Practice

1 Complete the table. Use ✓ for yes and ✗ for no.

Shape	Parallel lines	Perpendicular lines	Acute angles	Right angles	Obtuse angles

2 Look at this shape and fill in the blanks.

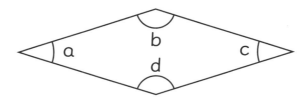

(a) How many angles does the shape have? ☐

(b) ☐ and ☐ are acute angles.

(c) ☐ and ☐ are obtuse angles.

Drawing 2D shapes

Starter

What can Elliott use to help him
draw these shapes?

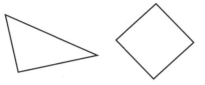

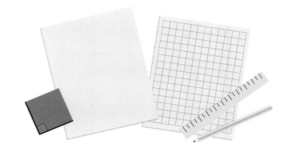

Example

Elliott draws a square using a
right-angle checker and a ruler.

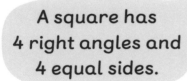

A square has
4 right angles and
4 equal sides.

He draws a triangle on squared paper.

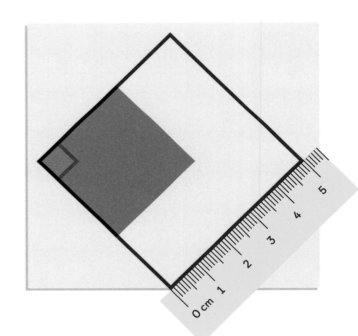

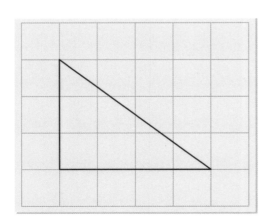

1 Use the 1-cm grid below to draw:

(a) a 5-cm square

(b) a right-angled triangle, with a horizontal side of 5 cm and a vertical side of 4 cm

(c) a rectangle that is 3 cm by 7 cm

2 Draw lines of symmetry through the shapes that are symmetrical.

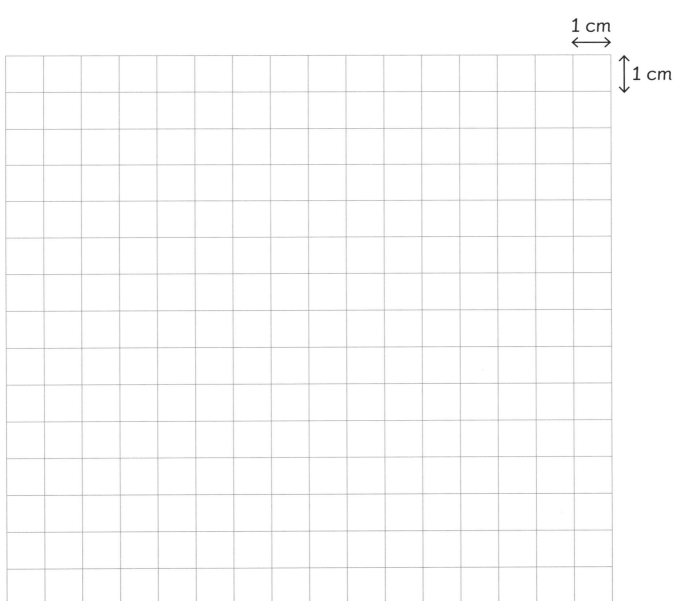

1 cm

1 cm

Making 3D shapes

Starter

What shape can we make by folding this net into a 3D shape?

A **net** is a shape that can be folded to make a solid.

Example

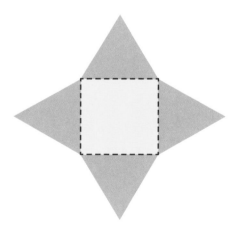

This is a **square-based pyramid.**

Emma folds the net so that the sides meet.

1   What shapes will these nets make?
Write **cube**, **cuboid**, **cylinder** or **triangular prism** for each net.

(a)

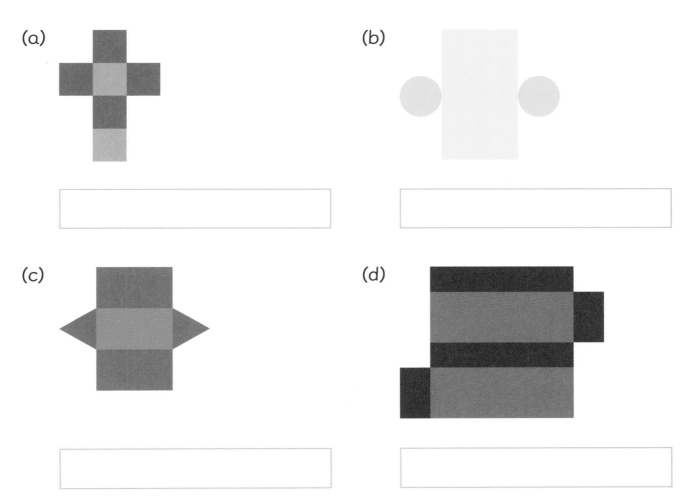

(b)

(c)

(d)

2   Circle the nets that will make a cube.

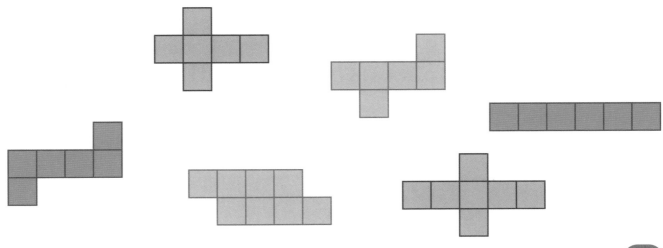

Describing 3D shapes

Starter

How can we describe these cuboids?

Example

This is a **face**.

All the faces are rectangles.

This is an **edge**. Edges are lines that connect two vertices.

A **vertex** is where two edges meet. The plural of vertex is vertices.

This is a special cuboid. All of its faces are squares. We can call this cuboid a cube.

I can see that there are parallel lines and perpendicular lines.

All cuboids have 6 faces and 12 edges.

A cuboid is a 3D shape where all the faces are rectangles.

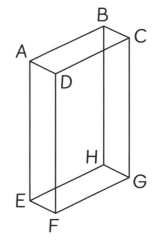

Look at the shape and fill in the blanks.

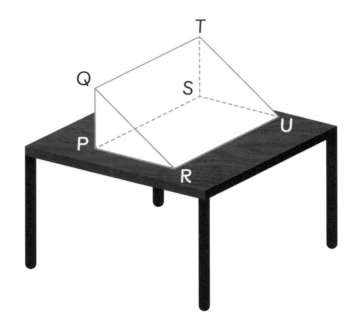

1 How many edges does this shape have?

2 Find 3 pairs of parallel lines.

3 Find 3 pairs of perpendicular lines.

4 (a) How many faces does this shape have?

(b) How many faces are triangles?

(c) How many faces are rectangles?

Measuring total length around a shape

Starter

Charles made a square from a 12-cm piece of wire.
Is it possible to make a rectangle from the same piece of wire?

Example

A square has four equal sides. Charles made a square with 3-cm sides from a 12-cm piece of wire.

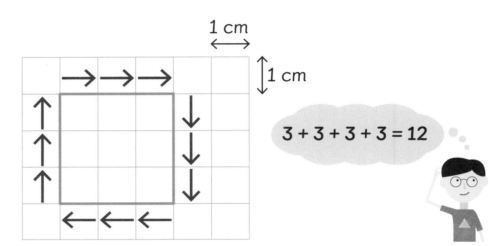

$3 + 3 + 3 + 3 = 12$

A rectangle has 2 longer sides and 2 shorter sides.
Charles also made this rectangle from the 12-cm piece of wire.
What is the length of each side?

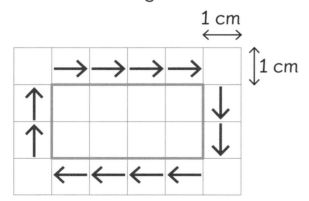

The total length around the edges of a shape is called the **perimeter**.

Add the lengths together.
$4 + 2 + 4 + 2 = 12$

Charles can make a square with 3-cm sides or a rectangle with sides of 2 cm and 4 cm from a 12-cm piece of wire.

What is the perimeter of each rectangle?

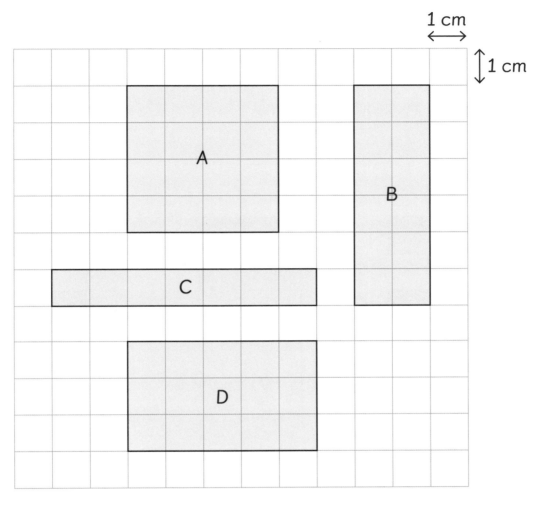

1 cm

1 cm

A

B

C

D

1 The perimeter of rectangle A is [ ] cm.

2 The perimeter of rectangle B is [ ] cm.

3 The perimeter of rectangle C is [ ] cm.

4 The perimeter of rectangle D is [ ] cm.

5 What do you notice about the perimeter of all of these rectangles?

Measuring perimeter using a grid

Starter

Do different figures made from 6 identical squares all have the same perimeter?

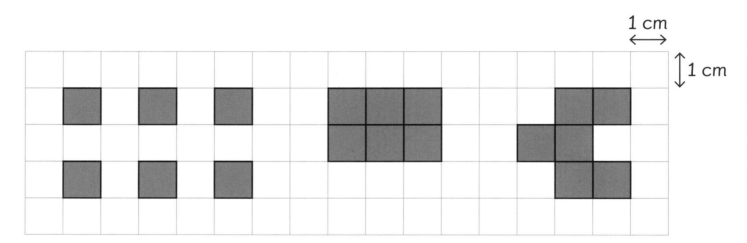

1 cm

1 cm

Example

This figure has a perimeter of 10 cm.

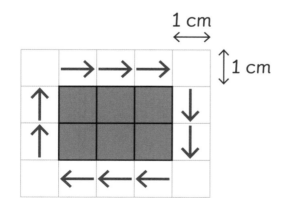

1 cm

1 cm

This figure has a perimeter of 14 cm.

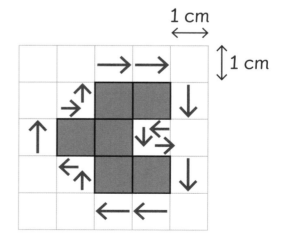

1 cm

1 cm

Both figures are made from 6 identical squares, but they have different perimeters.

1 Draw different figures by shading 5 squares next to each other. Draw as many as you can.

2 (a) Find the perimeter of each figure.

(b) What do you notice about the perimeters of the figures you made?

Measuring perimeters of complex shapes

Starter

How can we find the perimeter of this shape?

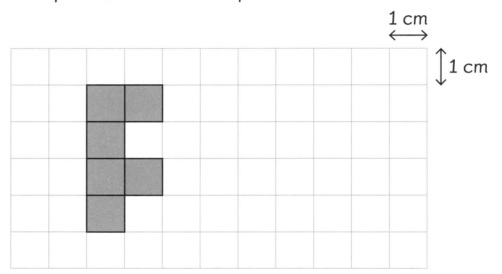

Example

Emma marks a dot to show where she starts counting.

I add the length of the sides until I get back to the dot.

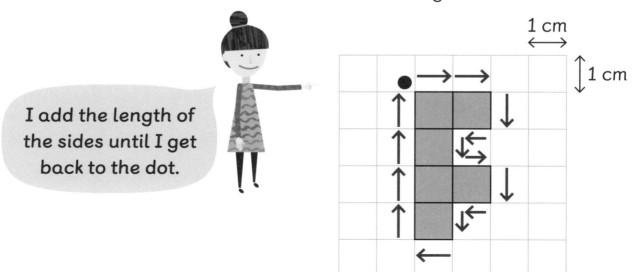

The perimeter of this shape is 14 cm.

Practice

Find the perimeter of each shape.

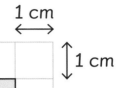

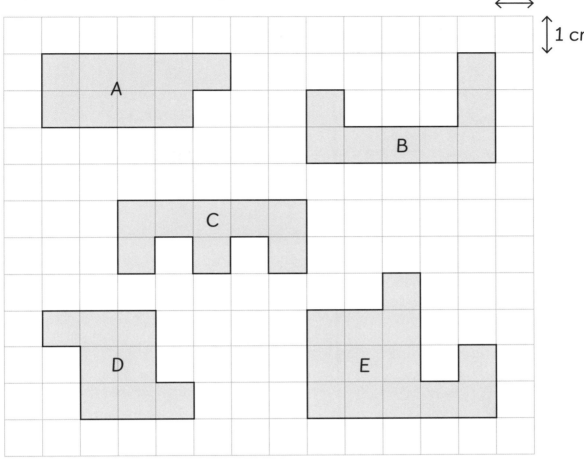

1   The perimeter of shape A is ⬚ cm.

2   The perimeter of shape B is ⬚ cm.

3   The perimeter of shape C is ⬚ cm.

4   The perimeter of shape D is ⬚ cm.

5   The perimeter of shape E is ⬚ cm.

Measuring perimeter using a ruler

Starter

How can we find the perimeter of the pentagon?

A pentagon has 5 sides.

Example

We can use a ruler to measure the sides of this pentagon.

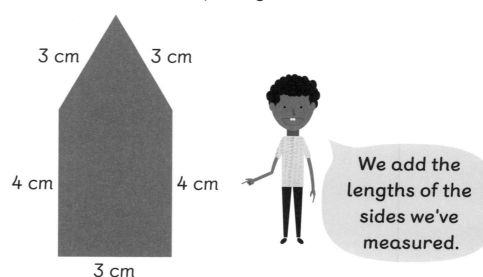

3 cm   3 cm

4 cm   4 cm

3 cm

We add the lengths of the sides we've measured.

3 + 4 + 3 + 4 + 3 = 17

The perimeter of the pentagon is 17 cm.

1 Use a ruler to find the perimeter of this shape.

Perimeter = ☐ cm

2 By measuring only two sides of this parallelogram, find its perimeter.

Perimeter = ☐ cm

3 Measure one side of these regular shapes to find their perimeters.

(a)

Perimeter = ☐ cm

(b)

Perimeter = ☐ cm

Calculating perimeters of regular shapes

Starter

How can we find the perimeter of this shape?

3 cm

Example

A square has four sides of equal length.
We only need to know the length of one side to find the perimeter.

3 + 3 + 3 + 3 = 12

The perimeter of the square is 12 cm.

4 × 3 = 12

For a rectangle, we need to know the measurements of a longer side and a shorter side.

5 cm

2 cm

2 + 5 + 2 + 5 = 14

The perimeter of the rectangle is 14 cm.

2 × 2 = 4
2 × 5 = 10

1 Find the perimeter of these regular shapes.

(a)

2 cm

Perimeter = ☐ cm

(b)

3 cm

Perimeter = ☐ cm

(c)

2 cm

Perimeter = ☐ cm

(d)

2 cm

Perimeter = ☐ cm

2 A square has a perimeter of 20 cm.
What is the length of each side of the square?

☐ cm

3 Find the perimeter of this regular octagon.

1 cm

Perimeter = ☐ cm

Calculating perimeters of complex shapes

Starter

Ravi's parents have an allotment where they grow vegetables. They want to buy some fencing to keep the rabbits from stealing their carrots.

How many metres of fencing do they need to buy?

Example

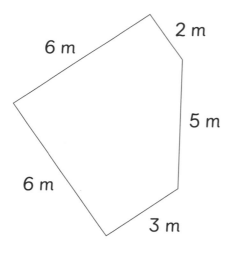

We need to know the perimeter. We can use a trundle wheel to measure the perimeter.

We need to add all the lengths to find the perimeter.

2 + 5 + 3 + 6 + 6 = 22

The perimeter is 22 m.

Ravi's parents need to buy 22 m of fencing.

Find the perimeter of each shape.

1

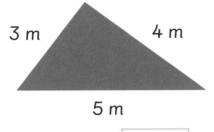

3 m   4 m

5 m

Perimeter = [   ] m

2

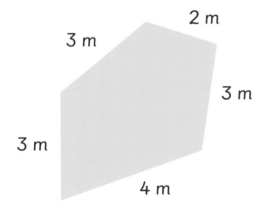

2 m

3 m

3 m

3 m

4 m

Perimeter = [   ] m

3

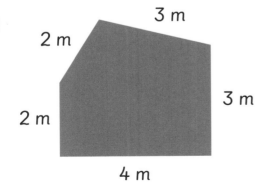

3 m

2 m

3 m

2 m

4 m

Perimeter = [   ] m

Review and challenge

1 Mark the right angles in the figure below.
How many right angles did you find?

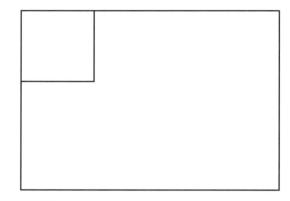

The figure has ☐ right angles.

2 Use quarter, half or three-quarter to describe each turn the figure has made.

(a)

The figure has made a ☐ turn clockwise.

(b)

The figure has made a ☐ turn anticlockwise.

(c)

The figure has made a [_____] turn anticlockwise.

3 Draw another line to make the following angles.
Mark each angle.

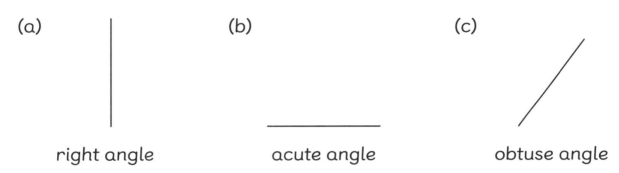

(a)   (b)   (c)

right angle   acute angle   obtuse angle

4 (a) Circle the shapes that have at least one pair of parallel lines.

(b) Colour the shapes that have at least one pair of perpendicular lines.

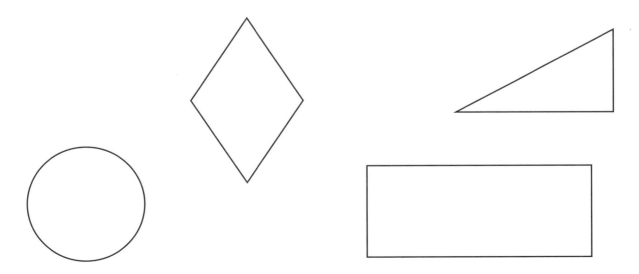

5 Look at the shape and fill in the blanks.

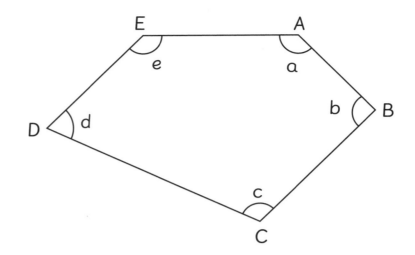

(a) Lines [ ] and [ ] are parallel lines.

(b) Angle [ ] is a right angle.

(c) Angle [ ] is an acute angle.

(d) Angles [ ] , [ ] and [ ] are obtuse angles.

6 Draw a square with 5-cm sides.

7 Draw a rectangle with sides of 3 cm and 6 cm.

8 How many faces, vertices and edges does each shape have?

		Number of faces	Number of vertices	Number of edges
cube				
cuboid				
square-based pyramid				

9 A rectangle has a perimeter of 20 cm.
One side has a length of 3 cm.
What are the lengths of the three other sides?

[ ] cm, [ ] cm, [ ] cm

10 Find the perimeter of this shape.

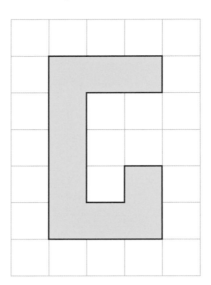

Perimeter = [ ] cm

11 Draw five different shapes each with a perimeter of 20 cm.

12 Charles cuts a rectangle in half like this:

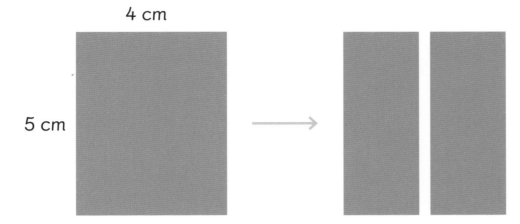

4 cm

5 cm

(a) What is the perimeter of the original rectangle?

The perimeter of the original rectangle is ⬚ cm.

(b) What is the sum of the perimeters of the two smaller rectangles?

The sum of the perimeters of the two smaller rectangles is ⬚ cm.

(c) Charles cuts the two pieces into halves. What is the sum of the perimeters of the four rectangles?

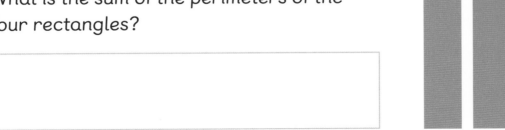

The sum of the perimeters of the four rectangles is ⬚ cm.

Answers

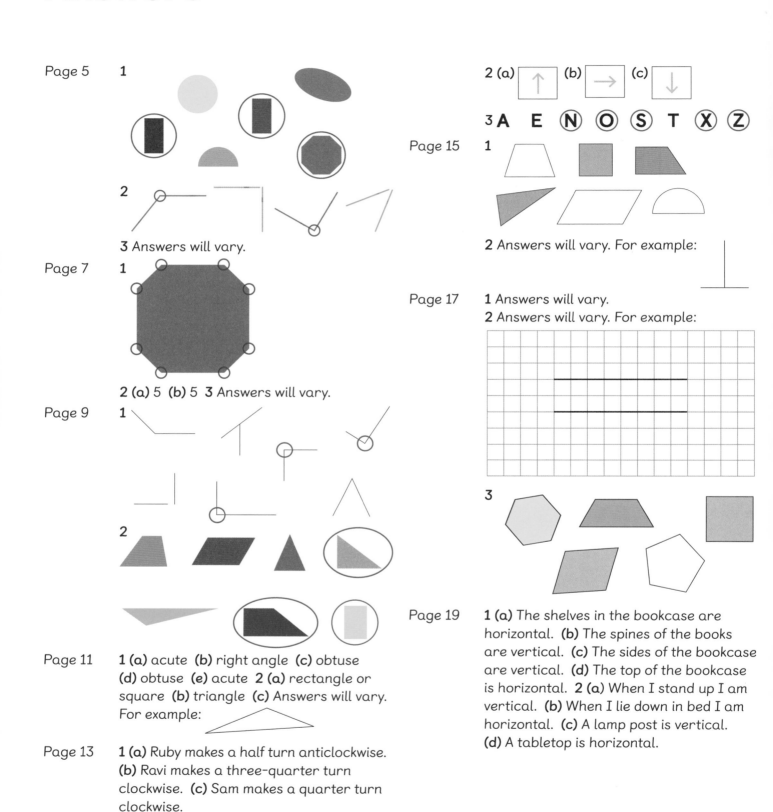

Page 5   1

2

3 Answers will vary.

Page 7   1

2 (a) 5 (b) 5 3 Answers will vary.

Page 9   1

2

Page 11   1 (a) acute (b) right angle (c) obtuse
(d) obtuse (e) acute 2 (a) rectangle or
square (b) triangle (c) Answers will vary.
For example:

Page 13   1 (a) Ruby makes a half turn anticlockwise.
(b) Ravi makes a three-quarter turn
clockwise. (c) Sam makes a quarter turn
clockwise.

2 (a) (b) (c)

3 A E N O S T X Z

Page 15   1

2 Answers will vary. For example:

Page 17   1 Answers will vary.
2 Answers will vary. For example:

3

Page 19   1 (a) The shelves in the bookcase are
horizontal. (b) The spines of the books
are vertical. (c) The sides of the bookcase
are vertical. (d) The top of the bookcase
is horizontal. 2 (a) When I stand up I am
vertical. (b) When I lie down in bed I am
horizontal. (c) A lamp post is vertical.
(d) A tabletop is horizontal.

Page 21 **1**

Shape	Parallel lines	Perpendicular lines	Acute angles	Right angles	Obtuse angles
◺	✗	✓	✓	✓	✗
☐	✓	✓	✗	✓	✗
⬠	✗	✗	✗	✗	✓
▱	✓	✗	✓	✗	✓

2 (a) 4 **(b)** a and c are acute angles.
(c) b and d are obtuse angles.

Page 23 **1**

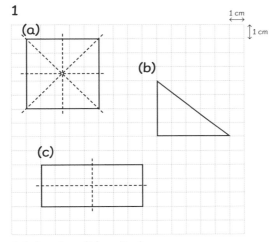

(a) (b) (c)

1 cm ↔   ↕ 1 cm

Page 25 **1 (a)** cube **(b)** cylinder
(c) triangular prism **(d)** cuboid
2

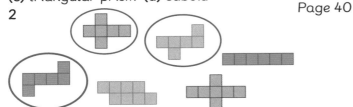

Page 27 **1** 9 **2** Possible answers: QP and TS, QT
and PS, PR and SU, PS and RU, QR and
TU, QT and RU **3** Possible answers: QP
and PR, QP and PS, PS and SU, PR and
PS, TS and SU, QT and TS, QP and QT,
PS and ST, PR and RU **4 (a)** 5 **(b)** 2 **(c)** 3

Page 29 **1** The perimeter of rectangle A is 16 cm.
2 The perimeter of rectangle B is 16 cm.
3 The perimeter of rectangle C is 16 cm.
4 The perimeter of rectangle D is 16 cm.
5 The perimeter of all four rectangles is
the same.

Page 31 **1** Answers will vary. For example:

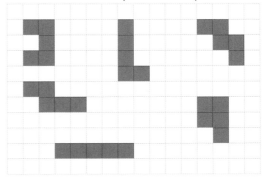

2 (a) The perimeter of each figure will
be 10 cm or 12 cm. **(b)** The perimeter of
each figure is either 10 cm or 12 cm.

Page 33 **1** The perimeter of shape A is 14 cm.
2 The perimeter of shape B is 18 cm.
3 The perimeter of shape C is 18 cm.
4 The perimeter of shape D is 14 cm.
5 The perimeter of shape E is 20 cm.

Page 35 **1** Perimeter = 11 cm
2 Perimeter = 18 cm
3 (a) Perimeter = 12 cm
(b) Perimeter = 10 cm

Page 37 **1 (a)** Perimeter = 8 cm
(b) Perimeter = 9 cm
(c) Perimeter = 10 cm
(d) Perimeter = 12 cm
2 5 cm **3** Perimeter = 8 cm

Page 39 **1** Perimeter = 12 cm
2 Perimeter = 15 cm
3 Perimeter = 14 cm

Page 40 **1**

The figure has
9 right angles.

2 (a) The figure has made a half turn
clockwise. **(b)** The figure has made a
three-quarter turn anticlockwise.

Page 41 **(c)** The figure has made a quarter turn
anticlockwise.

3 Answers will vary. For example:
(a)   **(b)**

(c)

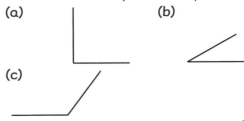

47

Answers continued

4 (a–b)

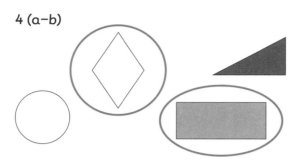

Page 42 **5 (a)** Lines BC and DE are parallel lines.
(b) Angle b is a right angle. **(c)** Angle d is an acute angle. **(d)** Angles a, c and e are obtuse angles.

6

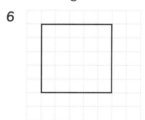

Page 43 **7**

8

		Number of faces	Number of vertices	Number of edges
cube		6	8	12
cuboid		6	8	12
square-based pyramid		5	5	8

9 3 cm, 7 cm, 7 cm

Page 44 **10** Perimeter = 22 cm
11 Answers will vary.

Page 45 **12 (a)** The perimeter of the original rectangle is 18 cm. **(b)** The sum of the perimeters of the two smaller rectangles is 28 cm. **(c)** The sum of the perimeters of the four rectangles is 48 cm.